BROADWAY PLAY PUBLISHING, INC.

BUBBLING BROWN SUGAR
A Musical Revue

Book by

Loften Mitchell

Based on a concept by

Rosetta LeNoire

249 WEST 29 STREET NEW YORK NY 10001 (212) 563-3820

BUBBLING BROWN SUGAR

Book Copyright 1985 by Loften Mitchell

First printing: May 1985

ISBN: 0-88145-26-X

Design by Marie Donovan
Set in Baskerville by L&F Technical Composition,
Lakeland, FL
Printed and bound by The Whitlock Press, Middletown, NY

PRODUCTION NOTES

This work may be presented with an elaborate set or with a very simple set. Originally it was designed to use chairs, tables, a stump for the Tree of Hope, and three steps in the upstage area. The use of lighting was recommended to assure fluidity of movement.

Actors may "triple" or "double" in roles. Members of the Ensemble have, in the past, played a number of roles. For example, the actress-singer-dancer playing Marsha has been seen as Young Irene. Tony, a white actor, has appeared in the Ensemble, as the Waiter, and as Dutch. Young Sage and Young Checkers were played by two members of the Ensemble. Dutch's Girl Friend and The Count were played by the actors who played Judy and Charlie.

All of this is simply noted here. It is not the intention of this author to dictate styles of presentation to management, directors, or choreographers. The one area where Rosetta LeNoire and this writer remain dogmatic is this: We have tried to create a family show without swear words, vulgarity, and with an emphasis on positive images.

1 November 1984   LOFTEN MITCHELL

CHARACTERS

MARSHA
GENE
BILL
TONY
NORMA
LAURA
SKIP
RAY
HELEN
NEWSBOY
FISHMAN
IRENE PAIGE
JOHN SAGE
CHECKERS CLARK

JIM
ELLA
WAITER
JUDY CANTRELL
CHARLIE PENDLETON
A WANDERING SON
GOSPEL LADY
YOUNG IRENE
YOUNG SAGE
YOUNG CHECKERS
BLUES SINGER
BUMPY JACKSON
COUNT
DUTCH
GIRLFRIEND

ACT ONE

SCENE ONE

(*Projections hit the screen as the OVERTURE is heard in its entirety. These are projections of prominent Harlem musical figures over the years.*)

(*When the projections end, the lights come up on a Harlem street. It is late afternoon of a day in the 1970s. We are at the corner of 131st Street and Seventh Avenue—now known as Adam Clayton Powell, Jr. Boulevard.*)

(*Music up. A light comes up on a young man, a dancer, who appears, looks around, searching, seeking. Another light picks out a young lady. The young man moves toward her and they begin to dance. Members of the Ensemble then appear and dance to an up-tempo number. The dance reaches a climax and the Ensemble sings out:* BUBBLING BROWN SUGAR.)

(*The music carries under. Members of the Ensemble crowd around in small groups, talking. These Ensemble members are:* MARSHA, GENE, BILL, TONY, NORMA, LAURA, SKIP, RAY, *and* HELEN.)

NEWSBOY: (*Enters*)   Papers! Papers! All papers here—
The Amsterdam News—loud and clear!
Columns by Billy Rowe and Sylvester
    Leaks—
Get your papers with all the news
So you don't end up with the Blues!

FISHMAN: (*Enters*)   Fry those porgies nice and brown,
Come on down—a dollar a pound!
Fishman, yay!
Fresh fish today!

MARSHA: I swear! You can't stand on a Harlem streetcorner for five minutes without somebody trying to sell you something!

GENE: Just be glad they ain't trying to sell you!

MARSHA: (*Hands on hips*) I ain't sure I appreciate that! (*Stops short*) Look out, everyone! Here she comes!

GENE: Better clear the street!

MARSHA: Looks like she got shot out of a cannon.

BILL: Which means only one thing——

TONY: She's looking for John Sage!

NORMA: I don't dig it. A big star like her, chasing that man! What does she see in him?

LAURA: A whole lot, I guess.

GENE: Cool it! Here she is!

(IRENE PAIGE *sweeps in. She is a tall, dignified, attractive woman, graying, but much younger-looking than her actual years.*)

ALL: Hi, there, Miss Paige!
         You look elegant!
         Yeah!

IRENE: Hi, kids! Marsha, come here, sweetheart. I want to ask you: Have you——

MARSHA: Have you seen John Sage?

IRENE: That's not funny!

MARSHA: I know. The story on the street is that you gave up Paris, Rome—a chance to be a countess—everything! Just to come back here and chase John Sage.

IRENE: Who's been saying that?

MARSHA: John Sage. That man thinks he is *sharp*!

IRENE: Tell the truth, he is. I'm working on making him dull—for everyone else.

MARSHA: He worries you.

IRENE: Yes. Because one time when I was a lot like you, he told me to stay away from downtown shows. He wanted us to build theatres around here. Well, I didn't listen—and we went separate ways.

MARSHA: (*Yelling to the others.*) Folks, I know the truth!

IRENE: There's more to it than that! I've seen Paris in the spring, London in the fall. And Rome. I've had it all, except —I don't know what all this means to you. The buildings. The people. And the streets. To me this is home.

(*Music. She sings* WHAT HARLEM IS TO ME.)

MARSHA: (*As the song ends*) Hey, y'all! Look who's moving!

(JOHN SAGE *and* CHECKERS CLARK *enter, carrying a trunk. At least,* SAGE *is carrying the trunk. He lifts his end, but* CHECKERS *is content to simply let his end drag along.*)

(SAGE *is a tall, thin, agile man, somewhat mystic, and he appears younger than his years.* CHECKERS *is tall, lanky, the same age as* SAGE, *but he has one genius and that is to do everything wrong.*)

SAGE: Checkers, will you please hold up your end of this trunk?

CHECKERS: John, if you pull your end, mine will follow.

SAGE: (*Drops his end.*) Ain't that brilliant? ? ?

MARSHA: Mr. Sage! Checkers! What y'all got in there?

LAURA: You're moving! You can't go moving out on us!

NORMA: Life 'round here wouldn't be the same without you all!

SAGE: Wait a minute! Wait a damn minute! We can all sing together, but damn if we can all talk together! We are not moving.

IRENE: Then where are you taking our old theatrical trunk, John?

SAGE: Schomburg Collection!

CHECKERS: Abyssinian Baptist Church!

SAGE: No wonder the trunk's so damn heavy. We're going in different directions. Look, it's just a prop trunk with a lot of old costumes and props that Checkers and I——

CHECKERS: The three of us.

SAGE: The three of us used to use in our shows.

MARSHA: (*Looking in trunk.*) Mr. Sage, you ain't got nothing in here but some old clothes. (*Takes out hat, holds it up.*) Look at this, you all!

LAURA: Let's see that!

IRENE: Give me that hat!

LAURA: Come on, Miss Paige! That hat looks like Methuselah's mother wore it!

IRENE: Is that so? Well, for your information that ancient bonnet belongs to me. I wore this hat when John Sage, Checkers, and I did *Sweet Georgia Brown* right over there at the Lafayette Theatre.

LAURA: When was that?

IRENE: A long time ago.

CHECKERS: A long, *long* time ago!

SAGE: Come on, Checkers. Let's get this thing to the Schomburg.

SKIP: The what?

SAGE: The Schomburg Collection for Black History and Culture.

CHECKERS: Where Harlem's history is kept, Brother.

(JIM *and* ELLA, *an attractive young couple, enter. She is full of enthusiasm, but he is tired.*)

JIM: Ella, I told you: I'm tired. I want to go home.

ELLA: Oh, come on, Jim. I just want to show you one more thing. This is the Tree of Hope.

JIM: That ain't no damn tree. It's a stump!

ELLA: Well, it used to be a tree.

JIM: I don't give a——(*Stops himself*) I don't care what it used to be. It's a stump now.

IRENE: What are you two going on about?

JIM: Aw, Miss Paige, would you believe my old lady is taking me on a out around my own home town. She's running my damn legs off—and now she's trying to tell me this stump is a tree!

SAGE: She's right. Jim. That's the stump to the Tree of Hope. When it was a living tree, it stood right over there——

IRENE: In front of the Lafayette Theatre.

SAGE: No, no. It stood between the Lafayette and Connie's Inn.

IRENE: A couple of inches don't make much difference.

SAGE: They don't, huh? You miss Heaven by a couple of inches and you'll land in Hell!

IRENE: I won't have to listen to your mouth if I do.

ELLA: Lord, you two been arguing since I can remember. Why aren't you married?

CHECKERS: I've been wondering the same thing myself.

SAGE: Stop wondering. A man should never marry a woman he loves. She'll drive him crazy!

IRENE: You can turn that around, honey. A woman should never marry a man she loves. He'll sit up on the Stool of Do Nothing and expect her to wait on him, hand and glove!

(*Naturally, the young ladies agree with her; naturally, the men groan in unison.*)

SAGE: Never mind all that! That tree stood right over there near the Lafayette—which is a church now.

CHECKERS: All Harlem's theatres are churches now—which shows that preachers and their congregations are better performers than Louis Armstrong, Bessie Smith, Butterbeans and Susie, and the three of us.

SAGE: You kids better listen to Checkers—sometimes.

IRENE: The tree got its name because one day a colored actor stood under it, hoping for work. A white manager came along and said he wanted to hire him. After that everybody and his mother stood under that tree, blocking the sidewalk.

CHECKERS: Then, when cars became more important than people, the city widened the street and cut down the tree.

SAGE: And Bill Robinson had the stump moved over here—for the people of Harlem. Read the inscription.

MARSHA: (*Reading*) "To the people of Harlem. You wanted a Tree of Hope, so here 'tis. Best wishes. Bill Robinson."

BILL: Bill Robinson! Bojangles! (*Music rises:* DOIN' THE NEW LOW-DOWN.) That man knew all the angles! He used to cut steps like this——

(*He dances with hands on hips as he imitates Mr. Robinson.*)

ELLA: Well! You know, he taught Shirley Temple how to dance! (*She joins* BILL *as they dance together.*)

SAGE: How about this one!

(*Music continues. He joins* BILL *and* ELLA *as they recreate one of Mr. Robinson's numbers. The music ends and the youngsters applaud.*)

JIM: You know, I've been passing this old stump for years, but I never knew it meant anything.

(*Music rises:* PATTER SONG.)

(*Following Chorus: Dance break.*)

JIM: (*Takes a hat from trunk.*) Look at this, Ella. Hey, whose is this?

IRENE: That's Checkers' tour guide hat.

JIM: Tours?

IRENE: When they weren't working as actors, they made money showing white folks around Harlem—for some pretty fancy fees.

JIM: How come they ain't rich?

IRENE: They weren't very good at it. John could never get his facts straight.

SAGE: That's a damn lie!

IRENE: And Checkers was forever getting lost.

CHECKERS: Signifying is worse than stealing or double dealing.

IRENE: There was only one thing they could count on to save the day.

SAGE: What's that?

IRENE: Me!

ELLA: (*Gets hat out of trunk.*) Look, Jim! An old top hat!

SAGE: That was Bert Williams' old hat.

ELLA: I read about him. He was a comedian!

SAGE: One of the greatest!

IRENE: John used to do a Bert Williams routine. Do it for the kids! Checkers, you set the scene.

CHECKERS: It is set! (*Then*) Bert was a great black actor. The first black star in an all-white Broadway show. He told a story about a poor man who was ordered by the law to drown his dog. Bert said: "I think I know how the man felt. I know I know how the dog felt!"

> He told another about a dude who was a dud.
> He joined the Darktown Poker Club
> And cursed the day they told him he could join
> For each and every night he'd contribute all his coin,
> So, he said:

SAGE: (*Has put on the old hat and now he sings out.*) I ain't never done nothing to nobody——(*Stops, talks over music.*) Now, Bert, when you play in that five card draw poker game tonight, you've got to play to win. And when you get that good hand, you've got to keep a poker face . . . Bert, don't grin.

(The music carries under. There follows Bert's famous Poker Game Pantomime. He deals imaginary cards. Five times around he deals, then puts down the imaginary deck. The drum punctuates these gestures.)

(He picks up his cards and glances at his imaginary companions. Now, he puts down his hand and deals the extra cards. He is pleased to give out three cards, curious when a player draws two, and filled with misgiving when someone draws one.)

(In the end he draws two for himself and we can see that these are just the cards he needs. Some lively betting starts. He becomes so confident that soon his whole stack of chips is in the pot.)

(Now comes the moment for the call. He prepares to rake in his winnings. But—there is a turn of events! He cranes his neck and looks. He has lost! His face and body become that of the saddest man in the world. He shoves his chips in the direction of the winner, then starts to move away, shoulders slumped. The music rises.)

IRENE: John, you took me back. Way back.

CHECKERS: When it was not safe to be black.

IRENE: You made me want to come out of retirement.

JIM: Mr. Sage, you make me admit: I wish I could have been there.

SAGE: You can! I'll take you there!

IRENE: Yes. We'll take you there.

SAGE: Ain't no way, Irene! You get back there in the past and you start digging downtown glamor—like you did before.

IRENE: Can't you forgive and forget?

SAGE: I can forgive, but I'll never forget . . . Checkers and I will take these kids on a tour through time and space . . . Don't you know the Legend of Harlem, Jim? The old folks say that just before the sun's setting a wisp of cloud floats across the sky, breaking off a single ray of light. You look straight at it and, if you believe hard enough, Time will stop still and take you back, back on a tour through time and space. Time will stop still and take you back, back on a tour through time and space. For, time in Harlem is a relative thing . . . A tour through time and space.

SAGE: And you'll get to know the beauty of the black black face.

CHECKERS: We'll give you a tour of the Harlem streets.

SAGE: You'll hear the sound of their intricate beats.

(*There is a sudden darkening of the stage as the wisp of cloud appears. A bright ray from the sun pours down. Music as* SAGE *raises his hands in a mystical fashion.*)

ELLA and JIM: What's happening, Miss Paige?

OTHERS: What's happening?

IRENE: You're going back—back in time . . .

(*A series of weird movements are performed by the Ensemble. The people all sway, helplessly, as they are transported back to the past. The lights fade as the music rises.*)

SCENE TWO

(*Music continues through the darkness. A spotlight picks out* BILL, *dressed in a 1920s costume. The music carries under.*)

(*Music.* BILL *sings* BACK TO MY TIME . . .)

(*The light fades on him and we fade into a downtown speakeasy during the 1920s.* JUDY CANTRELL *an attractive young white singer, is singing* SOME OF THESE DAYS *in a Sophie Tucker-like manner.*)

(SAGE, CHECKERS, JIM, *and* ELLA *sit at a table, listening while a* WAITER *stands not too far away, glaring at them. Over at a table near* JUDY *sits* CHARLES PENDLETON III, *a horn-rimmed, Ivy League-suited young man in his twenties.*)

JUDY: *Sings* SOME OF THESE DAYS.

JIM: Hey, man. Where are we?

SAGE: A speakeasy.

ELLA: Everybody around here seems so stuck up.

CHECKERS: This is a *downtown* speakeasy.

SAGE: We came to hear Judy Cantrell. The great Sophie Tucker's protégé—and one of the best. (*To* WAITER) Say, a round of drinks for my friends.

WAITER: We do not serve Negroes here.

SAGE: We do not eat or drink them. Scotches.

WAITER: That'll cost you fifty dollars a drink.

SAGE: Set up the house. (*Presents a credit card.*)

WAITER: What the hell is this?

SAGE: Bank Americard, man!

ELLA: Mr. Sage, we are not in the seventies.

SAGE: I know. That's exactly why I brought you here.

CHECKERS: Now they've had the experience. I think we ought to move to a more comfortable year.

JIM: We're not moving anywhere. I'm about to put this cat into orbit with his fifty-dollar drinks.

SAGE: Easy, Jim. You're a long way back.

JUDY: (*Approaches table.*) Hi, John! Hi, Checkers!

SAGE: Judy Cantrell!

CHECKERS: Hi, Judy. Sit down.

SAGE: Yeah. And have a fifty-dollar drink.

JUDY: A fifty dollar what? ? ? ?

WAITER: I don't make the rules around here.

JUDY: In a minute you're not going to be making a living around here, either.

JIM: Scotches, garçon!

(*The fuming* WAITER *goes out.*)

SAGE: Judy, our friends are Jim and Ella.

JUDY: Hi!

ELLA: Hello. We enjoyed your performance.

JUDY: You liked it?

JIM: It was out of sight!

JUDY: You didn't like it?

SAGE: No. He means you were great!

JUDY: He did like that?

JIM: Cool! Really cool!

CHECKERS: He means hot, really hot!

JUDY: Oh, thank you. We going uptown tonight?

SAGE: We got the places and the faces.

ELLA: So what're we waiting for?

CHECKERS: Someone to pay for it.

JUDY: Fellows, it's my treat! I got a rich date: Charles Pendleton the Third. Right over there! (*She waves to him.* CHARLIE *waves back.*) Charles is very proper, but he's cute—and what the hell, he's loaded!

CHECKERS: Tell him to join the party.

SAGE: (*As* JUDY *goes for* CHARLIE.) Now, you kids cool it till we find out where this cat is coming from——

JUDY: (*Returns with* CHARLIE.) Charlie, I want you to meet my two Harlem favorites, John Sage and Checkers Clark. And Jim and Ella, right? . . . Charlie went to Harvard, but he likes people anyway.

(*The* WAITER *returns with drinks, serves them.*)

JUDY: You folks get acquainted. I'm going to slip into something comfortable. (*She goes.*)

CHARLIE: (*Sitting*) Well, here we are! Cheers! Down the hatch! (*They drink.*) I must say my dad would have a spasm if he saw me talking and drinking with colored folks.

(JIM *nearly spits up his drink.*)

CHARLIE: Don't get me wrong! I think it's swell. It's just that my dad thinks I'm too liberal for my own good . . . Say, I do hope colored is the correct terminology.

SAGE: Oh, we've been called all kinds of things.

CHARLIE: That must be very confusing. Waiter, we'll have another round, please.

CHECKERS: These cost fifty dollars a drink, you know.

CHARLIE: Fifty dollars a drink? That's peculiar. (*Pulls out a roll of bills.*) Will this cover it?

SAGE: I don't know. But, it sure makes it less peculiar.

CHARLIE: Judy tells me we're going up to Harlem. Hit the spots. Do a little slumming. I think that's quaint.

JIM: You ever been to Harlem, Charlie?

CHARLIE: No. Never.

SAGE: We're going to show you fifty years of Harlem and all in one night.

CHARLIE: Fifty years of Harlem in one night! Wow! Is this some kind of Black Magic?

(*The others gulp in unison.*)

CHARLIE: Judy tells me a retainer would be in order for this tour. I hope this will be enough. (*He puts a roll of bills on the table.* CHECKERS *promptly picks up the roll and pockets it.*)

CHECKERS: Mr. Pendleton, I think you're going to find this to be a most comfortable tour.

SAGE: Just don't let my share get too damn comfortable in your pocket.

JUDY: (*Reappears, clothes changed.*) All right, everybody. I'm ready. Let's go.

CHARLIE: Judy, I can hardly wait. What is Harlem really like?

JUDY: It's a lot like Harvard.

CHARLIE: Harlem's like Harvard?

CHECKERS: Yeah! It'll cost you a bundle, but you get one hell of an education!

(*They get ready to leave.*)

SAGE: I got the tip.

(*Music. He sings* NOBODY.)

(*During the song,* SAGE *has taken a roll of bills and held these out to the* WAITER. *Now, as the* WAITER *reaches,* SAGE *sticks the bills back into his pocket and walks out, leaving the* WAITER *emptyhanded. The lights fade.*)

SCENE THREE

(*The streets of New York. Music carries under as the lights fade in.*)

(BILL *leads* SAGE, JUDY, CHARLIE, JIM, *and* ELLA *as they move to the music:* STROLLING.)

(*The music carries under as they stop at a corner.*)

SAGE: Harlem. This is Harlem.

JUDY: Well, Charlie. What do you think of my Harlem?

(*Music up. The Ensemble enters. Members are paired off into couples and they perform the* STROLLING *routine.*)

JUDY: Well, Charlie?

CHARLIE: Quaint. Really quaint! What is that they're doing?

JIM: Ask them.

CHARLIE: Excuse me, sir. Exactly what is that you're doing?

GENE: Strolling, man. Strolling!

JIM: Break that on down for him, Brother.

GENE: You walk with your right leg dipping a bit, resembling a limp. Now, dig this.

(*He demonstrates. The Ensemble follows suit and the Dance begins.*)
    Stroll, man, Stroll, and walk that broad—
    That old walking broad.
    Stroll this way and that way and then you sway!
    It must be jelly 'cause jam don't shake that way!

(*The Dance continues to a rousing climax and the Ensemble exits.*)

JUDY: Come on, Charlie. Try it.

(*Music. She breaks into the Charleston.* CHARLIE *tries it and nearly falls down.*)

SAGE: Come on, Charlie!

CHECKERS: Come on, Charlie!

(CHARLIE *finally "gets" the steps. He and* JUDY *dance, then he nearly collapses.* JIM *and* CHECKERS *grab him and hold him up. The lights change.*)

SCENE FOUR

(*The scene is 135th Street and Lenox Avenue. They all stop.*)

CHECKERS: Lenox Avenue, everybody!

ELLA: Looks like 135th Street.

SAGE: Right!

JIM: So this is what my hometown used to look like! Nice!

CHARLIE: Jim, look! A subway!

JIM: What's the big deal? It's an ordinary subway stop.

SAGE: No, Jim. That's no ordinary subway. This is the Grand Central Station of Harlem. Folks came up out of there with all their hopes for a new life. That's why this subway stop is called——

JUDY: The Pearly Gates!

SAGE: I see you know your Negro history. (*Then*) It was also called one of the stops on the Underground Railroad.

ELLA: My mother grew up on this block. She came here when she was fifteen.

SAGE: Folks all over the world know you get to New York, find that "A" train, and take it home to Harlem.

(*Suddenly,* IRENE *appears on an upper level, yelling from the present.*)

IRENE: Hold on now! Hold on! What're you telling these folks? The "A" train does not now and never did go to Lenox. The "A" train's on the Eight Avenue line.

SAGE: Irene, I told you—we are conducting this tour. You stay the hell up there in the seventies where you belong!

IRENE: Not while you're mixing up the twenties!

SAGE: I could get as mixed up as an omelet and not be as mixed up as you were on the day you were born.

IRENE: I had to be mixed up to get mixed up with you!

(*The light fades on her.*)

CHARLIE: Jim! Jim, a train's coming!

SAGE: Newcomers arriving. Artists, writers, scholars, home folks with dreams trot up these steps with a million schemes. And many a wandering child rode this train. Coming back to Harlem. Coming home again.

(*From out of the subway stop the people pour—all kinds of folks, looking around for relatives, looking at the big buildings, looking, looking. And then a* WANDERING SON *comes up the steps, singing* I'M GOIN' TO TELL GOD ALL MY TROUBLES.)

(*The* WANDERING SON'S *mother, the* GOSPEL LADY, *starts singing to him. As she sings, she moves into center stage and the others join her.*)

(*Music:* HIS EYE IS ON THE SPARROW.)

(*At the conclusion of this number* SAGE *and* CHECKERS *are standing upstage. The others have gone.* YOUNG IRENE PAIGE *steps out of the station. She resembles the Ensemble member we know as* MARSHA. *She wears a long cape and that old, old hat we saw in the first scene of the play.*)

IRENE: Mr. Sage! Mr. Sage! (*To* SAGE) I'm looking for a man named John Sage. He was supposed to meet me here and take me to the Lafayette Theatre.

(*Before* SAGE *can answer two young men appear. They are* YOUNG SAGE *and* YOUNG CHECKERS.)

YOUNG SAGE: I'm John Sage.

YOUNG IRENE: Oh, am I glad to see you?! I'm Irene Paige.

YOUNG SAGE: You're—Irene Paige?

YOUNG CHECKERS: Don't look at me, man. You hired her!

YOUNG SAGE: This is my partner, Checkers Clark.

YOUNG IRENE: Checkers Clark! I'm going to be in a show with Checkers Clark!

YOUNG CHECKERS: That's your new Georgia Brown, huh? Hired sight unseen! Good luck!

YOUNG IRENE: Mr. Sage, I've got to tell you: I've been out on the road, getting rave reviews in bad shows. Now, you've called me here to New York to play Georgia Brown. What I'm trying to say is: I sure hope this is going to be a good show. It will be, won't it?

YOUNG SAGE: Are you kidding? With me in it?

YOUNG CHECKERS: And me!

YOUNG IRENE: And me!

(*She moves upstage as the music*—SWEET GEORGIA BROWN —*rises. She looks out on Harlem, then begins to remove her cape and hat*—*revealing herself as a strikingly attractive young lady.*)

(*She starts singing and* YOUNG SAGE *and* YOUNG CHECKERS *join her in a pulsating dance number.*)

(*The Dance continues. At its conclusion the three dance off. Music carries under.*)

SAGE: Irene. That was the beginning. Of magical moments.

IRENE: Golden days, glorious days.

SAGE: Georgia Brown tore up the town. Then there was that show we did, From Dixie to Broadway.

IRENE: That was with Florence Mills. And remember our big Alhambra hit.

SAGE: Remember the song.

IRENE: Yes, I remember.

(*Sings:* HONEYSUCKLE ROSE.)

(*Repeat/up tempo*—SAGE *and* IRENE. *Following* HONEY SUCKLE ROSE.)

SAGE: That was our act. Oh, yeah!

IRENE: Remember what we used to do for an encore up at my place?

SAGE: Come on, honey! I got to tend to business. I promised to show Charlie and Judy this old town. And I got to keep an eye on Checkers so he don't mess with my half of the money.

IRENE: John, forget the money. Come back with me.

SAGE: Forget the money? Are you crazy?

IRENE: I guess I was crazy to think anything could bring us back together.

SAGE: I'll be back as soon as this tour is over.

IRENE: How long is that?

SAGE: About thirty years.

IRENE: Thirty years? Knowing you, it'll take you that long to get the icicles out of your veins!

(*She turns and dashes out.* CHARLIE *and* JUDY *rush in.*)

SAGE: Come on, kids. Time for the hot spots. It's nighttime and it's white time!

CHARLIE: Nighttime and white time? What does that mean?

SAGE: It means white folks get colored in a hurry. Come on!

(*They rush out as the lights fade.*)

SCENE FIVE

(*The Night Club Tour.*)

(*Music up. Loud, brassy. Lights flood the stage. Projections flash, indicating the names of night clubs. These include: "101 Ranch", "Connie's Inn", "Dickie Wells'", "Saratoga", and other places.*)

(CHARLIE *and* JUDY *dance in and out of these places. At Connie's Inn a Female Blues Singer is spotlighted, singing* STORMY MONDAY BLUES.)

(*Piano music carries under as she continues singing.*)

(*The lights fade, then come up on three male singers. They sing* ROSETTA, *and they appear at other times during this scene. The last time they appear they are, to put it mildly, drunk and ready to collapse.*)

(*Now a male singer appears in a night club setting. He resembles our* JIM *and he sings in Billy Eckstine fashion as a Dance Team performs.*)

(*At the end of the dance number, the man leaves the woman on stage, dancing by herself as the song continues.*)

(*The lights fade. They come up on the three male singers.*)

(*Lights fade. Music up:* ST. LOUIS BLUES. *Projection: "101 Ranch." *SAGE *and* CHECKERS *appears, costumed as* RUSTY *and* DUSTY.)

DUSTY (SAGE): Man, I didn't know that was you.

RUSTY (CHECKERS): I didn't know that was you either. I sure am glad to see you. Do you know who I just saw? I . . .

DUSTY: Saw him yesterday. You know what he told me? He . . .

RUSTY: Told me that too. But you know what I think? I . . .

DUSTY: Think so too. Only I'm worried be . . .

RUSTY: Don't worry about that. But do you know what I hear? I . . .

DUSTY: Heard that too . . . But she's a good girl. She goes to bed every night at nine o'clock. Gets up at four o'clock and goes home.

RUSTY: Man, you know what I like about running into you? A man can always get into a good conversation.

(*They sing* IN HONEYSUCKLE TIME.)

(*They dance off. The three singers return, drunk.*)

(*Lights fade. Now lights come up on a quartet, singing* SOLITUDE.)

(*The song ends and the lights fade out.*)

SCENE SIX

(*A street corner.* SAGE, CHECKERS, CHARLIE, *and* JUDY *enter.* SAGE *and* CHECKERS *flop themselves down on the midsection.*)

CHARLIE: This place flows with energy!

JUDY: It's alive! Alive!

CHECKERS: And I'm half dead.

CHECKERS: This is hardly the New York City people talk about.

SAGE: If the New York City people talk about really existed, Hell would be out of business!

(ELLA *and* JIM *rush in, excited.*)

ELLA: Hi, everybody! You should've been with us!

SAGE: I'm just glad you're here. I thought Checkers had lost two more customers.

JIM: We dug the Savoy!

ELLA: Now, I know what my mother's been talking about for years!

JIM: I have dug the track, and I'm going back! Come on, Mr. Sage, let's hit it!

SAGE: Mr. Sage is showing his age.

JIM: Checkers?

CHECKERS: I'm like the fox. I am beat to my sox.

JIM: All right, Charlie and Judy, I'll show you the Savoy myself. Let the old folks rest.

CHECKERS: What did he call us?

SAGE: He called you old folks.

CHECKERS: I got my second wind. Savoy, here we come!

(CHECKERS *rushes out with* JIM, ELLA, CHARLIE, *and* JUDY. SAGE *stands there, looking after them, smiling.*)

(*A crash of cymbals.* BILL *appears on an upper level, dressed as a zoot-suiter*)

BILL: (*As music carries under.*) Come on up and dig the Savoy! Do the Flat Foot Floogy with the Floy Floy! It's a killer-diller from Manila. It's a solid sender, a real mindbender. It is hip as a whip and mellow as a cello. Come on up to Jive Time and dig my rhyme!

(*The music rises as* BILL *moves off.*)

SAGE: Damn Sam! I've never been to the Savoy without Irene.

(*A pretty lady crosses the stage. His eyes follow her.*)

Hell, there's always the first time. Sorry, Irene.

(IRENE *appears on an upper level.*)

IRENE: Wait a minute there, John Sage!

(SAGE *freezes.* DUTCH, *an obvious downtown mobster, appears with his henchman,* COUNT.)

DUTCH: Miss Paige! Irene Paige! We have an offer for you: The Cotton Club—and some downtown contracts. Money and more money.

SAGE: It's—happening—again.

IRENE: No, John. Not this time! Listen, Dutch—you can take your offer and keep it this time. And if I weren't a lady, I'd tell you where to shove it! (*Walking down to* SAGE, *takes his arm.*) You are taking me to the Savoy!

SAGE: Time is, indeed, a relative thing. It does change things!

(*They go off, arm in arm, as the music rises.*)

SCENE SEVEN

(*The Finale. Inside the Savoy.*)

(*Music up: This is a medley* (SAVOY, ACT ONE), *primarily of* STOMPIN' AT THE SAVOY *and* TAKE THE A TRAIN. *Couples swarm over the dance floor, doing the Lindy Hop and variations of it. As the scene progresses, a circle forms and one couple and then another move into the center and dance.* SAGE, IRENE, *and* CHECKERS *are standing on an upper level, clapping hands.*)

(GENE *grabs* IRENE *and leads her into the circle. They do a number of intricate steps. On the Break,* IRENE *gets herself lost in the crowd and moves back to where she was standing.*)

(*The music becomes furious and driving now. The dancing reaches a rousing climax and as it comes to an end, the Ensemble yells:*)

ENSEMBLE: Savoy!

(*Hands are held out in the direction of the audience. The lights fade out.*)

CURTAIN

END OF ACT ONE

ACT TWO

SCENE ONE

(*Musical interlude* (SAVOY, ACT TWO))

(*The lights come up outside the Savoy.* BILL *steps into center stage and sings.*)

(*Members of the Ensemble pour out onto the stage.* CHECKERS, CHARLIE, *and* JUDY *are among the group.* CHECKERS *leads* CHARLIE *and* JUDY *off.*)

GENE: Man, that was a gasser and a blaster!

NORMA: We gonna stomp down that place one of these days!

GENE: Yeah! Did you see the floor shaking under Laura's feet when she hopped?

LAURA: Honey, that was not me! That was that peroxide blonde you cut a rug with.

(JIM *and* ELLA *step out of the Savoy and stand, listening.*)

NORMA: Talk to him, girl. I did not appreciate the way Mr. Skip pranced around, either.

SKIP: Aw, Norma, if you'd gotten any closer to that baldheaded dude, you'd have been behind him!

NORMA: Never mind the baldheaded dude! That broad you danced with will never bump her chin opening a door!

(*She does an imitation of a high-chested women.* JIM *and* ELLA *laugh.*)

GENE: You newcomers sure got in the act.

JIM: It was a moment in history!

(*Music rises. He sings:* BUBBLING BROWN SUGAR.)

(*The song ends.* JIM *and* ELLA *embrace. The others start out.* GENE *stops, gives* JIM *and* ELLA *two cards.*)

GENE: We're digging a House Rent Party. Fall on over. You're gonna need these cards to get in.

JIM: All right! We will dig that scene later.

GENE: Swinging!

(*He goes.* JIM *begins* TRUCKING *and humming snatches of* STOMPIN' AT THE SAVOY.)

ELLA: Well! Look at who's having a good time!

JIM: Ella, I love this place!

ELLA: And you weren't interested in our history!

JIM: The only history I ever heard was rhetoric. Words, words, words—which didn't mean a thing. But, seeing it, hearing it, reaching out and touching it! Seeing the Tree of Hope alive and well! I'm going to hate to see this end.

ELLA: It won't end—as long as there's you and me. (*She sings* LOVE WILL FIND A WAY.)

(*They embrace as the song ends.* SAGE *and* IRENE *have entered.*)

IRENE: Isn't that pretty?

JIM: Hey! How long have you two been standing there?

SAGE: Long enough to hear that revolutionary song!

IRENE: It is revolutionary. When that song was written, it was taboo for Blacks to make love on stage.

SAGE: We weren't supposed to be able to mate romantically. You were supposed to say: "Come here, baby, or I'll break your damn neck! Pow!"

IRENE: (*As the youngsters laugh.*) Come on. Let's get on with the tour.

ELLA: Charlie and Judy went with Checkers.

SAGE: That means just one thing.

JIM: What's that?

SAGE: They are lost.

(BUMPY JACKSON *enters. He is a smartly dressed man of middle years.*)

BUMPY: Excuse me, folks—

SAGE: Bumpy!

BUMPY: John! Irene! Good to see you!

IRENE: (*As* BUMPY *kisses her hand.*)

SAGE: Ain't he busy.

BUMPY: Sorry, John, but—she is fine as wine!

IRENE: Oh, I do love a man who tells the truth!

BUMPY: Listen, I'd love to stay and talk, but I have unfinished business to take care of. You understand? I suggest you all stand clear. There may be some action here.

SAGE: Sure. Sure. Nice bumping into you, Bumpy!

(BUMPY *moves upstage, stands in the shadows.*)

ELLA: Who was that?

IRENE: Bumpy Jackson. One of the top numbers racket men in all Harlem.

ELLA: Yes. I've heard of him!

JIM: Bumpy? How'd he get a name like that?

SAGE: If we don't do like he says, we may find out! Come on!

(*They get out of there. The* COUNT, DUTCH'S *henchman, appears, looks out but does not see* BUMPY.)

COUNT: All clear, Boss.

(DUTCH *and his* GIRLFRIEND *enter.*)

GIRL: Gee, Dutch! I had a terrific time.

BUMPY: Dutch! Hey, Dutch!

DUTCH: Oh! It's you—

BUMPY: Yeah.

DUTCH: What's on your mind, Bumpy?

BUMPY: The same thing that's on your mind. The numbers.

DUTCH: Hey, what're you talking about?

BUMPY: You know what I'm talking about. Prohibition is dead. You're out of the liquor business.

DUTCH: Yeah. The government's taken crime off the street and put it in Washington where it can be controlled. Ha, ha, ha!

(*He gives out with a laugh. The* GIRLFRIEND *and the* COUNT *join him.* DUTCH *raises his hand, waves it as he stops laughing. The other two follow suit, abruptly.*)

BUMPY: I just want to tell you, Dutch, that if you're looking for a new line of work, don't look towards Harlem and the numbers.

DUTCH: If that's what you're worried about, forget it. We're just out for a little fun. Taking my friends to the Cotton Club.

BUMPY: We don't like that, either. The Cotton Club doesn't welcome my people. We let it stand because it hires my folks.

DUTCH: O.K., Bumpy. We can talk this whole thing over. Come on. I'll buy you a drink. Tell your friends to come along.

BUMPY: My friends are with me. (*He pats his pocket.*) Now, hear me well, Dutch. The first person to cross 110th Street with any idea about the numbers is going to get a very warm welcome from all my friends. (*Pats pocket again.*) Remember what Omar said.

DUTCH: Yeah. He's got a great act.

BUMPY: "The moving finger writes, and having writ, moves on. . ." (*He goes out.*)

GIRL: Huh! Who does he think he is?

COUNT: Shut up! Boss, that guy means business! If you put out a contract on him, it better not be written with vanishing ink.

DUTCH: (*Sings* DUTCH'S SONG.)

(*The music stops. He goes out with the* GIRL *and the* COUNT. JIM, ELLA, IRENE, *and* SAGE *reenter.*)

ELLA: What was that all 'bout?

IRENE: About the way the downtown boys took over our numbers racket.

SAGE: Two weeks from now one of Harlem's biggest numbers bankers will have a run on his bank. He'll borrow from Dutch and Dutch will be in from then on.

JIM: Why couldn't he just borrow from a Brother?

SAGE: Jim, when I can answer that question, oak trees will grow out of my grave!

ELLA: We'll continue this at the party. Listen (*Reads from card.*):

> Come on down where the Chicks are mellow
> And Chicks can pick up a real fine fellow.
> You eat pig's feet and drink hearty
> At a Social Whist Party:
> 141 West 131 Street Apartment L . . ."
> (*Stops*)
> It's going on now.

SAGE: You kids go. And have a good time!

(JIM *and* ELLA *dash out.*)

IRENE: I'm glad you let 'em go. That Savoy did me in.

SAGE: Honey, you were ready as a radio!

IRENE: You wore me out!

SAGE: Baby, if I'd married you in my twenties, I'd have been dead before I was thirty. That would've been one hell of a trip to heaven!

IRENE: (*Being cute.*) I'll bet you told that to all the girls while I was away.

SAGE: I should have, but didn't. (*Music. He sings:* AIN'T MISBEHAVIN'.)

(*The song ends.* SAGE *and* IRENE *are in an embrace.* CHECKERS *rushes in:*)

CHECKERS: John! John! Man, am I glad to see you. I can't find them white folks. I have looked and looked, so—I came to ask you to help.

SAGE: (*Still embracing* IRENE.) Man, go away! I am taking care of business.

CHECKERS: Well, speaking of business: Charlie only paid me part of the fee. That part he didn't pay was *your* share.

SAGE: (*Crashes to Earth.*) This damn fool has lost my money! (*To* IRENE.) Honey, come on and let's take care of my unfinished business, then we can take care of *the* business.

IRENE: Checkers, you are out to lunch!

CHECKERS: You two can't afford to join me unless you catch up with Charlie!

SAGE: Stupid! Stupid! (*As he and* IRENE *leave.*) Stupid!

CHECKERS: (*Thinks about this.*) He's right! (*Then*) I may lose people. I may even lose my mind. But, there's one thing I will not lose. That's the beat!

(*Music rises:* PRAY FOR THE LIGHTS TO GO OUT.)

SCENE TWO

(*The scene is a street corner.* CHARLIE *and* JUDY *wander in.*)

CHARLIE: Oh, Judy! What a fantastic night!

JUDY: Charlie, it has to be! Wandering around Harlem with you.

CHARLIE: I'm sorry we keep getting lost. That Checkers——

JUDY: Don't be sorry. I almost wouldn't mind staying lost.

CHARLIE: Let's arrange that.

JUDY: You know, when this evening started I wondered who was taking who for a ride. But, now—it's more like flying.

CHARLIE: I know how you feel.

JUDY: You do?

CHARLIE: Sure. Because I'm feeling things I never felt before.

JUDY: It's this town. It does things to you.

(*Music is heard in the background.*)

CHARLIE: It makes things happen inside. Listen. Listen: It seems as though music is coming out of the buildings.

JUDY: Charlie, the music is coming out of the buildings. Up there. See! That's a House Rent Party.

CHARLIE: A—what?

JUDY: A rent party. Rent! Don't you know what that is? Gosh! Everybody I know pays rent.

CHARLIE: Well, everybody I know collects it!

(*They stand there as the lights come up on the House Rent Party. A piano is playing* (HOUSE RENT PARTY). *People are milling around, talking and dancing.* JIM *and* ELLA *enter.*)

LAURA: Well! Let the house get raided!

NORMA: (*Holds up a can.*) Everybody! Just in case you all can't read. This says: "Feed the kitty." The kitty's meowing 'cause she ain't been fed yet. Got to feed it till we get up the rent.

JIM: Where're those pig's feet and greens? Huh?

NORMA: You folks ain't paid nothing yet.

GENE: This here is a rent party! You got to help raise the rent or raise the roof!

OTHERS: Yeah! . . . Got to pay! . . . Yeah!

ELLA: Hold on now. I'm gonna buy us a piece of this party.
(*She sings:* I GOT IT BAD.)

NORMA: (*As the music ends.*) Well, honey! I sure hope my landlord was listening!

(*The piano continues (Lead-in). Lights dim out on the party, then come up on* CHARLIE *and* JUDY *on the street.*)

JUDY: Charlie, the beat! It's everywhere. In the air you breathe. My head dances to it.

CHARLIE: I'm dancing, too.

(CHARLIE *begins to dance, then he turns somersault.*)

JUDY: Charlie, what's gotten into you? Please! That is not proper!

CHARLIE: Judy, I have been acting proper all my life and living improperly. And it has been absolutely dull.

JUDY: With all your money? Why?

CHARLIE: No color.

(*The music rises* (PRELUDE). *He sings* HARLEM MAKES YOU FEEL.)

(*The number ends.* JIM *and* ELLA *rush in. Enthusiastic greetings follow.*)

JIM: Charlie! Judy!

(*They all try to talk at the same time.* JIM *holds up his hand.*)

Wait a minute, wait a minute! We can all sing together, but damn if we can all talk together.

CHARLIE: That's clever, Jim.

JIM: Thanks.

ELLA: We thought you all were lost. What happened to you?

JUDY: Something wonderful.

CHARLIE: We were uptown.

JUDY: Way uptown!

ELLA: So were we.

CHARLIE: Downtown will never be the same again.

JIM: Charlie, after tonight nothing's gonna be the same!

CHARLIE: You ain't just jiving, man! Dig this: While we were lost tonight, Judy and I saw the cutest little brownstone. 138th Street and Seventh Avenue! We're going to buy it.

JIM: On Strivers' Row?

CHARLIE: Is that what they call it? Well, you and Ella can just drop in any old time.

JIM: Now that we know how to deal with the Time Zone, we will do just that!

CHARLIE: Fab-u-lous! I sure dig this scene!

JIM: Well, all right, Charlie!

CHARLIE: Well, all right, Jim!

(JIM *holds out his palm.* CHARLIE *gives him "some skin"—only* CHARLIE *is heavy handed.* JIM *blows on his burning palm.*)

ELLA: Well, say it again.

JIM: All right, Charlie.

CHARLIE: Well, all right, Jim.

JIM: (*Holding out palm.*) Easy now.

(CHARLIE *brings his hand down with great gentility. Both laugh.* CHECKERS *enters, then* IRENE *and* SAGE.)

SAGE: Well, well! How nice we can all be together again!

ELLA: Where do we go next?

SAGE: A night is not a night until you've been to Paradise.

CHECKERS: Small's Paradise.

(*Music gliss. Voices are singing "Harlem, Sweet Harlem"* (SMALL'S PARADISE) *as the lights change.*)

SCENE FOUR

(*The lights come up on Small's Paradise.* JIM, ELLA, SAGE, IRENE, CHARLIE, JUDY, *and* CHECKERS *are at a table.* BILL *appears as master of ceremonies.*)

BILL: Brown sugar bubbles and by now you know why:
Some things are eternal, they never ever die!
Small's Paradise is a legend all its own
It survives the years and goes on and on.

(*Sings* JIM JAM JUMPIN' JIVE.)

BILL: Yes indeedy, yes indeedy. We got the thing for all you needy. We've paid off the cops—so we're gonna pull out all the stops. Now, don't let a soul let out a cough, 'cause we're gonna spin our propellers and take off.

Now before I bring on some of our stars, I want to tell you something that happened the other night. A new chorus girl walked in here with a new mink coat!

I say, "Where'd you get your new mink coat?"
She says—"From my new boyfriend."
I say, "Didn't you have to do anything?"
She say . . .

IRENE: "Oh, just shorten the sleeves a little."

(BILL *does a double-take as the others laugh.*)

BILL: Now—speaking of horses, I had a dream the other night. All night I kept seeing the number Five. Number Five all night long. I woke up at five o'clock. I walked over to Fifth Avenue. I took the Number Five bus to the race track. Waited for the Fifth Race. Went to Window Number Five and bet five dollars on Number Five. And you know what?

JIM: He came in fifth!

(BILL *does another double-take as the others laugh.*)

BILL: Well, since all our non-paying guests know all our paying routines, we'll move right along . . . Folks, we got enough stars here to light up another sky. And two of them you've got to meet and greet: Irene Paige and John Sage. And, who knows, someday if I live long enough, I may hear that Miss Paige has changed her name to Mrs. Sage.

SAGE: Time does change things.

(IRENE *now steps forward and music rises.*)

IRENE: I have been on a memory trip—beautiful this time because memory edits, filters, and rearranges things. My memories have brought awaking skies . . .

(*She sings* MEMORIES OF YOU.)

(*The song ends. The others applaud.* IRENE *goes to* JIM *and* ELLA.)

IRENE: Are you kids having a good time?

ELLA: Oh, yes! We wish we could stay here in the past!

SAGE: You can't. And it's just as important that you look to the future. And when you do, remember this:

(MARSHA *appears and the music rises. She sings* GOD BLESS THE CHILD.)

(MARSHA *leaves the stage. As the song ends.* JIM *stands, raises his glass.*)

JIM: And now as we return to our time, let's toast yesterdays on which we build our todays and tomorrows. A toast and a song!

(*As music rises, he begins to sing* DON'T MEAN A THING.)

(*The Ensemble members enter, stop as the cymbals are heard. They tap back in response, then stride forward.* BILL *and* MARSHA *tap over and join the Ensemble members.*)

(*A series of intricate dance steps are performed as the music becomes pulsating. This reaches a rousing climax as the lights fade out.*)

CURTAIN

THE END